The Miraculous Medal

as revealed to St Catherine Labouré

by Lady Cecil Kerr

Revised and updated by
Raymond Edwards

*All booklets are published thanks to the
generous support of the members of the
Catholic Truth Society*

CATHOLIC TRUTH SOCIETY

PUBLISHERS TO THE HOLY SEE

Contents

All rights reserved. Published 2015 by The Incorporated Catholic Truth Society, 40-46 Harleyford Road London SE11 5AY Tel: 020 7640 0042 Fax: 020 7640 0046. First published 1930; revised 1934, 1948; very frequently reprinted. This edition newly revised 2015 by Raymond Edwards. Copyright 2015 © The Incorporated Catholic Truth Society.

ISBN 978 1 78469 036 6

Introduction

The Church of God, like every other living body, has her ups and downs, her seasons of prosperity and adversity. At one time the flame of faith burns high, fanned, maybe, by the storms of persecution; at another she is swept by a burst of missionary zeal; or, unfortunately, she passes through a barren age when fervour wanes and saints are few. One such bleak and dreary period was the eighteenth century, chilled as it was by the blight of Jansenism and the cold teachings of the rationalists. Even apparitions of the Blessed Virgin Mary stopped for the space of a century; but she had not forgotten her children. And, as proof of her affection, she offered them a token - a medal, with the promise that those who wore it would receive a shower of graces. So generously were her promises fulfilled that the medal quickly won the title of "Miraculous".

The 27th day of November 1930 marked the centenary of this precious gift, and 28th May 1933 saw the solemn beatification of Sister Catherine Labouré to whom the medal was entrusted by Our Lady. Two decades later, on 27th July 1947, Sister Catherine was canonised with all due solemnity. Now, almost two hundred years after the first appearance of the Miraculous Medal, it may not be inopportune to retell its history, for, much as it is loved by Catholics, few, perhaps, know much about its origin.

Zoë Labouré

In the year 1806, a little girl was born in a village on the Cote d'Or in France. She was one of a large family - seven boys and three girls - and was named Zoë Labouré. Her parents were simple farmers, pious and hardworking, owners of a small farm and vineyard which enabled them to bring their children up in peace and plenty. Then, when Zoë was only eight years old, sorrow came to them; her mother died, and the little girl turned in her grief to Our Blessed Lady, asking from then on to be her child. She and her sisters were sent for a time to an aunt, but two years later their father brought them home, wishing himself to supervise their education. Zoë made her first Communion at the age of twelve and on that day resolved to devote her life entirely to God. Her older sister, who had long desired to become a Sister of Charity, was now allowed to follow her vocation, and from then on the care and responsibility for the household devolved upon little Zoë. Industrious and unselfish, she was well capable of the task, and accepted her heavy duties as a mere matter of course. A woman was brought in to do the rougher work, but the child herself cooked for the family and undertook the general management, and every day, her housework done, she would trudge off to the fields to carry their dinner to the labourers. But her favourite occupation was the care of a huge colony of seven or eight hundred pigeons. She knew them all and, at the first sound of her call, the whole flock would swoop down on her, almost burying her in the snowstorm of their rustling wings. Her only outside pleasure was an occasional visit to a neighbouring convent of the Sisters of Charity, where she found a sympathetic friend in the Superior, but, with characteristic reserve, even with her Zoë did not share her desire to devote herself to God. And, indeed, she herself did not as yet know what form this desire was to take. Her deep piety was obvious to all: winter and summer found her kneeling long hours on the cold floor of the church absorbed in prayer; and, not satisfied with her arduous life, she practised considerable asceticism in secret, fasting rigorously every Friday and Saturday - a habit of which her father strongly disapproved when he discovered it.

God has a plan for you

And then, one night, she had a dream. She found herself in church where an old and venerable priest was saying Mass. She attended the Mass with much devotion, and when the priest had finished, he turned and beckoned her to come to him. Struck with fear, she left the church, walking backwards, her eyes still fixed on him. On her way home, still dreaming, she went to visit a sick friend.

Here, again, she found the same old priest, and this time he spoke to her. "It is a good thing, my child, to care for the sick," he said. "You shrink from me now, but the day will come when you will rejoice to come to me. God has a plan for you. Do not forget this." Surprised and still more afraid, she left the house, and it seemed to her she floated home, her feet not touching the ground. As soon as she reached her father's house, she woke up, but she could not throw off the deep impression of her dream. Sometime afterwards she accompanied her sister-in-law to a convent of the Sisters of Charity, and there in the parlour hung a picture of the old priest she had seen. Deeply agitated, she asked who it was, and was told, "St Vincent." From that time on, she had no doubt about her vocation, but the way was not yet clear. Her father, who had already given one daughter to the convent, refused to let her go; instead, he sent her to visit one of her brothers, who ran a large restaurant in Paris. If he hoped this would distract her from her purpose he was sadly disappointed, for this glimpse of the great world made her only the more anxious to enter the convent. After a time, her sister-in-law came to her assistance, acting as mediator with her father, with the result that, in the year 1830, at twenty-four years of age, she was allowed to enter the mother house of the Sisters of Charity, in the Rue du Bac in Paris.

Sister Catherine

Here she found as her spiritual director a wise and saintly man, Fr Jean-Marie Aladel. He soon began to see that God was leading this young Sister along unusual ways, and he watched her closely. To all outward appearance she was a very ordinary Sister of Charity, a typical daughter of St Vincent, hardworking, self-effacing, full of practical common sense. Her superiors reported her as a good, steady girl with no striking qualities or outstanding capabilities. The secrets of her inner life remained her own, revealed to no one but her director.

The first of the mysterious events with which God favoured her took place a few days after her arrival. It was the occasion of the solemn translation of the relics of St Vincent, and Sister Catherine, as she was henceforth to be called, was praying with great fervour to her holy patron, when, as she says in a letter to Fr Aladel:

> I had the consolation of seeing St Vincent's heart, just above the case which contains his relics. It appeared to me on three consecutive days in the same place. The first time it was white, and I understood this to mean peace, tranquillity, and concord. The second time it was of a fiery hue, the symbol of the charity which was to

Sister Catherine Labouré.

revive and extend throughout the world. Lastly it was red and black which seemed to fill me with sadness. I was overcome with fear and heard a voice which said: "The heart of St Vincent is deeply afflicted at the great calamities which are about to overwhelm France."

On the last day of the feast (which like many celebrations at that time extended over eight days), she again saw the heart, this time of a light red colour, and the interior voice said: "St Vincent's heart is somewhat consoled. He has obtained from God, through the intercession of Mary, that his two families [this meant the Daughters of Charity, and his own order of men, the Congregation of the Missions or Vincentian Fathers] shall not perish in the midst of these calamities, and that God will make use of them to revive the Faith in France."

Forebodings

Not a little disturbed by these strange happenings, Sister Catherine reported them to her director, who told her to put them aside and think no more about them. However, the divine favours did not cease. It would appear that at this time she had a very strong sense of the presence of Jesus in the Blessed Sacrament: "Except," as she wrote, "if a doubt crossed my mind, when I ceased to behold him, on account of the effort to examine what I saw, for fear of being deceived." Our Lord showed himself under different forms according to the feast. On Trinity Sunday, she saw him as king with a cross upon his breast. At the reading of the Gospel, the cross and other royal insignia fell at his feet, and she was filled with the sad conviction that great calamities were about to befall France, and that the king would be dethroned - as did, indeed, shortly afterwards take place (see the following section). She foretold several other similar events, and Fr Aladel could not fail to be struck by the accuracy of her predictions.

Sister Catherine and the Blessed Virgin

Sister Catherine's great desire in life was to see Our Blessed Lady, and she constantly begged her Guardian Angel and St Vincent for this favour. On 18th July, the eve of St Vincent's feast, she went to bed convinced that her holy patron would obtain her wish. About half-past eleven she woke up hearing her name called out three times. Looking through her curtains she saw a lovely child, about four or five years old, with golden hair and dressed in white. Bright rays surrounded him, illuminating the whole room. "Come," he said, "come to the chapel. The Blessed Virgin is waiting for you." Sister Catherine hesitated, thinking to herself: "The other sisters will hear me and I shall be found out."

"Don't be afraid," said the child in answer to her thought. "They are all asleep. I will go with you." Sister Catherine quickly dressed and followed him. To her surprise she saw that all the lamps were lit, and when they reached the chapel door it opened to them. The chapel itself was brilliantly illuminated, as though for Midnight Mass. The child led her to the altar rails, where she knelt down, while he stood within the sanctuary. It seemed to her that they had waited a long time when, at midnight, the

The Chapel of Our Lady of the Miraculous Medal in Paris is more commonly referred to by its address, "140 Rue du Bac".

child spoke again: "Here is the Blessed Virgin. Here she is," he said, and Sister Catherine heard a faint rustling as of a silk gown. Looking up she saw a lady of extraordinary beauty enter the sanctuary and sit down in the priest's chair. Her appearance and clothes - a white robe and blue veil - were like those worn by St Anne in a picture which hung in the chapel, but her face was different. As Sister Catherine hesitated, uncertain what to think, the child spoke again in a stern voice and asked her if the Queen of Heaven were not free to appear in any form she pleased. At these words, Sister Catherine's doubts vanished and, throwing herself upon her knees, she clasped her hands upon Our Lady's lap as though she were indeed her own mother. What followed is best told in her own words.

The vision

At that moment I experienced the sweetest feeling I had ever known. Our Lady explained to me how I was to act in all my difficulties, and, pointing to the altar with her left hand, she told me to go there and open my heart, that there I would receive all the consolations I should need, and then she added: "My child, I have a mission to entrust to you. You will have to suffer much in the performance of it, but the thought that it will be for the glory of God will enable you to overcome all your trials. You will be opposed but do not be afraid. Grace will be given you. Tell everything that takes place with simplicity and confidence. You will see certain things, you will receive inspirations in prayer. Give an account of everything to him who has charge of your soul."

I then asked the Blessed Virgin what was the meaning of certain things which had been shown me. She answered: "My child, the times are evil and misfortunes are about to overwhelm France. The throne will be destroyed and the whole world convulsed by all sorts of calamities."

[*The French King, Charles X, was deposed at the end of July 1830, and replaced by his distant cousin, Louis Philippe of Orléans, who was not in the direct line of succession. Louis Philippe was himself deposed in 1848, and the Second Republic inaugurated. This lasted until 1851, when Bonaparte's nephew seized power and declared himself Emperor Napoleon III.*]

The Blessed Virgin looked very sad as she said this. "But," she added, "come to the foot of this altar. Here graces will be poured out on everyone, on anyone who asks for them, great or small. There will come a time when danger will be great and it will seem that all is lost. But have confidence. You will feel that I am with you and that God and St Vincent are protecting the two communities [*again, this refers to the Vincentian Fathers and the Daughters of Charity*]. Have confidence, do not be discouraged, I shall be with you." Then with tears in her eyes Our Lady continued: "There will be victims in other communities. There will be victims among the clergy of Paris. The Archbishop will die. My child, the cross will be despised and trodden underfoot. Our Lord's side will be pierced anew; the streets will run with blood, and the whole world will be in sorrow."

Protection and assurance

At these words Our Lady seemed overwhelmed with grief, and Sister Catherine thought to herself: "When will this happen?" An interior light revealed to her that they would take place in forty years' time. In fact, these predictions were fulfilled when the Commune, a revolutionary committee, seized power in Paris in 1871 after France's defeat by Prussia. Numerous hostages, including the Archbishop of Paris, were killed by the Communards when the Army retook the city. The Sisters, however, were wonderfully protected throughout.

Then Our Lady gave her several messages for Fr Aladel and again assured her of her constant protection: "My eyes are always watching you, I shall grant you many graces. Special graces will be given to all who ask for them, but people must pray."

"I cannot tell," adds Sister Catherine, "how long I remained with the Blessed Virgin. All I know is that after speaking with me for some time she vanished like a shadow." The Sister then rose from her knees and found the child still standing in the same place. "She is gone," he said, and led her back to the dormitory, the light shining round him as before. She was convinced it was her guardian angel.

Sister Catherine duly told this vision to Fr Aladel, only to be received, as before, with apparent incredulity; but nonetheless, he was observing events closely.

The Miraculous Medal

Then, on 27th November, there came the crowning vision for which all these others had merely been the preparation. Sister Catherine was making her evening meditation in the chapel about half-past five, when she heard the familiar sound of rustling silk, and again Our Lady stood before her. She was of middle height, beautiful beyond description, and dressed in a robe "white as the dawn". Her head was covered with a white veil that fell to her feet, and she stood on a globe. In her hands she held another globe and, as she presented it to Our Lord, she raised her eyes to heaven and her face became transfigured.

"Suddenly," Sister Catherine said, "her fingers were covered with rings, set with rare precious stones, from which sprang rays of such brilliance that her feet and robe were no longer visible. The stones were of different sizes and the rays varied in their brilliance. I cannot tell all I felt or how much I learnt in that short space of time. As I gazed upon her, the Blessed Virgin bent her eyes on me and a voice spoke in the depths of my heart: 'This globe which you see represents the whole world, and France in particular and each person individually.' I know no words to express the beauty and brilliance of

The Miraculous Medal.

the rays as Our Lady added: 'Behold the symbol of the graces I bestow on those who ask for them.'"

Sister Catherine explained later that some of the stones gave out no rays, and these she understood to represent the graces for which we forget to ask.

The vision of the Medal

"I cannot tell whether at that moment I was alive or not," she continued, "all I know is that I was happy. Gradually there appeared around Our Blessed Lady a sort of oval frame on which was written in letters of gold: 'O Mary conceived without sin, pray for us who have recourse to you.' This prayer formed a semicircle, beginning on a level with her right hand and ending on a level with her left. Then it seemed as though the frame turned round, and I could see at the back of it the letter M, surmounted by a cross with a bar below, and underneath the hearts of Jesus and Mary, the one surrounded with a crown of thorns, the other pierced by a sword. As I looked the voice spoke again: 'Have a medal struck according to this pattern. Those who wear it will receive great graces, especially if they wear it round their necks. There will be abundant graces for those who have confidence.'"

Some weeks later Sister Catherine was favoured with another vision very similar to the first, only this time Our

Lady, instead of remaining in the sanctuary, went and stood behind the tabernacle on the very spot where her statue has since been placed. She looked to be about forty years of age. The vision was repeated a third time, and this time Fr Aladel, who up till then had heard the story with apparent indifference, asked Sister Catherine what was written on the back of the medal. She answered that she had seen nothing. "Well," he said, "ask Our Lady what should be written there." After she had prayed for a long time, she heard a voice say: "The M and two hearts speak plainly enough." Two very popular devotions, the Sacred Heart of Jesus and the Immaculate Heart of Mary, are thus combined in the Miraculous Medal. When Our Lady next appeared to Sister Catherine, she told her it was for the last time. "My child," she said, "you will not see me anymore, but you will hear my voice during your prayers."

A simple faith

Fr Aladel's delay in fulfilling the wishes of Our Lady was a sad trial to the young Sister. With her simple faith and her certainty as to the genuineness of her visions, she could not understand his prudent hesitation. Yet it never occurred to her to consult anybody else. The secret was her Blessed Mother's, and the message was for Fr Aladel alone, and even to him she never spoke of it except when urged by an irresistible impulse. Nor were her visions allowed to interfere in any way with the duties of her busy life. Only one occasion has been recorded, when, on coming from the chapel to the refectory, she was so absorbed as to leave food untouched upon her plate. "Are you still in ecstasy, Sister?" said the superior, little guessing how near her words came to the truth.

Word spreads

And now Sister Catherine's year of novitiate was up, and the time had come for her to leave the mother house and the chapel made so dear to her by her heavenly Mother. And still Our Lady's commission remained unfulfilled! But, poor Sister, what more could she do? She was sent to the Hospice at Enghien where Fr Aladel continued to act as her director. She little knew how closely he was watching her, so as to test the truth of her revelations. He had already sought advice from several of his superiors, though of course without mentioning her name. Rumours were also beginning to spread among the community that one of the Sisters was seeing visions; everyone was understandably very curious who it was. One day a number of the Sisters were besieging Fr Aladel with questions. Here, he thought, was an opportunity of testing Sister Catherine, and he watched her narrowly. Perfectly self-possessed, she joined in the conversation with such simplicity as entirely to divert attention from herself.

Seven months after Sister Catherine's arrival at Enghien, Our Lady again spoke to her, complaining that her commands had not been carried out. "But, Mother," cried Sister Catherine in distress, "you know he doesn't believe me." "Do not fear," was the reply, "the day will come when he will do as I desire. He is my servant and he will be afraid of offending me."

Sister Catherine duly repeated this conversation to Fr Aladel, who felt that the time had indeed come to act. "If Our Lady is displeased," he said to himself, "it cannot be with the sister, who clearly can do no more. It must therefore be with me."

The Medal is Struck

Deeply troubled in mind, Fr Aladel took an opportunity of laying the whole matter before the Archbishop of Paris, Mgr de Quelen. Having listened with close attention to the story, the Archbishop declared that there was nothing in it contrary to the faith and that he could see no reason why the suggested medal should not be made, adding that he wanted the first one sent to himself. Fr Aladel was overjoyed, and at once took steps for the production of a medal as described by Sister Catherine, bearing the image of Our Lady on the one side and the monogram with the two hearts on the other. Archbishop de Quelen was determined to put it to the test. He was very worried about the spiritual condition of the former Archbishop of Malines, who was close to death. This man, Dominique Dufour de Pradt, had been one of Napoleon Bonaparte's chaplains, but had resigned his see after Waterloo and entered French politics as a liberal. Archbishop de Quelen armed himself with the medal, and went to M. Dufour's house, only to be refused admittance. However, soon afterwards he received a message of apology, begging him to return. The dying man then confessed his sins and, having retracted all his former errors, received the last sacraments and died peacefully in the Archbishop's presence. Mgr de Quelen, filled with joy, rushed to Fr Aladel to tell him the happy news, which he attributed to the medal.

Fr Aladel himself at once took a medal to Sister Catherine, who received it with the greatest devotion and respect. After such long delay and so many contradictions, her Blessed Mother's wish had been fulfilled at last. Joy filled her heart.

The fulfilment of Our Lady's promises

"Now it must be spread," she said. And spread it was to a degree which must have equalled her highest expectations. It spread like wildfire, and stories of the marvellous effects which accompanied it - graces, cures, conversions - poured in from every side. The wonders of this medal were discussed everywhere. Fr Aladel brought out a little pamphlet relating its history, but the medal itself was its own greatest proof: it was the medal which worked miracles, and as the Miraculous Medal it has been known ever since.

With overflowing heart the humble Sister watched this glorious fulfilment of Our Lady's promises, at the same time happy that she herself remained unknown. Now and again she would bear a further message from Our Lady to Fr Aladel: at one time it was to tell him to set up an altar in the convent chapel, commemorating the apparitions. "Many graces will be attached to it," she told him, "and will fall abundantly on yourself and the community." Again, she told him to pray especially for spiritual favours, assuring him that if he asked with confidence, he would obtain all he wanted. Another message led to still more worldwide consequences, resulting in the foundation of the many confraternities of Children of Mary that have done so much good. "The Blessed Virgin wishes you to found a congregation of which you are to be superior," said Sister Catherine. "It is a confraternity of Children of Mary. Our Blessed Lady will shower down graces upon them and you, and indulgences will be granted them." Sister Catherine also foretold that keeping May as the month of Mary would become a general devotion throughout the Church, and that March as St Joseph's month would also receive due honour.

Miracles of the Medal

All the time, the Miraculous Medal continued on its triumphant way. Fr Aladel has described how rapidly it spread.

"The medals of the Immaculate Conception were propagated in a truly marvellous manner, among all classes and in all provinces," he writes. "We received the most consoling accounts from every side. 'They are reviving fervour in both town and country,' we are assured by priests, themselves filled with the spirit of God; while distinguished prelates testified to their sure confidence in these medals which they looked on as a means designed by Providence to revive the enfeebled faith of our century. And truly they are re-awakening it day by day in many hearts in which it seemed extinct. They are restoring peace and unity in families rent with discord; in fact, none of those who wear them fail to feel their salutary effect. In all parts of France there appears a growing eagerness among the faithful of all ages and conditions to procure the Miraculous Medal. Indifferent Christians, hardened sinners, Protestants, unbelievers, Jews, beg for it, receive it with delight, and wear it with devotion. Nor is it propagated in France alone: it has spread rapidly over Switzerland, Italy, Spain, Belgium, England, America, the East, reaching as far even as China. In Naples, no sooner was it known than the Cathedral chapter made application for it at one of our houses; the king had a number struck in silver for himself and his court and family, and ordered a million for distribution during the outbreak of cholera, with the result that it is held in honour in nearly every house and many of the churches. In Rome the Generals of the religious Orders took active part in the propaganda, while the Holy Father himself placed the medal at the foot of his crucifix and gave it to people as a special token of his blessing."

Archbishop de Quelen showed no less zeal in distributing it among the sick and suffering whom he visited, and, he said, it never failed to bear good fruit.

Up to this time, the medal had not received canonical approval for veneration, and so that this might now happen, a court of inquiry was set up to make formal examination into the medal's origin. The court held nineteen sittings, the principal witness being Fr Aladel. As for Sister Catherine herself, nothing would induce her to come forward. She had told her spiritual director everything, and had nothing more to say; and it really seemed that Our Lady was in league to protect her for, when further pressed, she found that for the time being all memory of the apparitions had vanished from her mind. The judges saw her humility as a proof of the genuineness of her revelations, but the most conclusive testimony was the marvellous stream of graces which still continued to accompany the medal. Finally, the ecclesiastical authorities, although they made no pronouncement as to the reality of the visions, gave formal approval, both to the medal itself, and to pictures and statues of Our Lady as described by Sister Catherine.

Revival in the Church

But medals and images are merely symbols - it was the increase in devotion to Mary Immaculate herself which was the point, and this revelation of Our Lady to the humble Sister was a seed destined to bring forth much fruit. There was no more wholehearted apostle of the cause than Mgr de Quelen, and it was in answer to his request that Pope Gregory XVI gave permission for the solemn celebration of the feast of the Immaculate Conception, and also for the addition of the invocation *Regina sine labe originali concepta*, ("Queen conceived without original sin") to the Litany of Loreto. We have already mentioned the confraternities of the Children of Mary and their far-reaching results; a further development, which few people connect with the visions of Sister Catherine, is the now famous shrine of Notre Dame des Victoires in Paris.

Many miracles

In Paris at that time there was a priest called Fr Desgenettes, who was among the most enthusiastic promoters of the Miraculous Medal. In fact he strongly urged the Daughters of Charity to open the chapel of the apparitions to the public, so it might become a place of pilgrimage, but they refused, declaring such fame to be contrary to the spirit of St Vincent. Then Fr Desgenettes was moved to a new parish where he found things in a terribly bad way. Surrounded by theatres and stock exchanges, his parishioners had little use for religion, and the church was practically empty. It was only by persistent effort that the new parish priest could obtain admittance to the dying, and then only in secular dress and often after it was too late. Four years of apparently fruitless labour so disheartened him that he was on the point of resigning his post when, one morning as he was saying Mass, he heard an interior voice say to him "Consecrate your parish to the holy and immaculate heart of Mary", and he was overwhelmed with a feeling of great peace. He drew up some statutes for a confraternity and submitted them to the Archbishop who was happy to approve them, and authorised the formation of an "Association of the Immaculate Heart of Mary for the Conversion of Sinners". A meeting was called which Fr Desgenettes expected at most sixty to attend. To his amazement, eight hundred people came, among them a large number of men, and the new association was founded amid scenes of great enthusiasm. Fr Desgenettes attributed this blessing to Our Lady and he chose the Miraculous Medal as the badge of the associates. For many years afterwards, Notre Dame des Victoires reigned as Queen in Paris, the sure refuge of her people in all times of storm and trouble - and not in Paris only, for anxious hearts called to her from many distant lands, and not in vain, as may be seen from the countless thanks offerings which decorate her shrine. Nevertheless, despite the growing glories of his church, Fr Desgenettes remained faithful to his early love, and whenever he found a Sister of Charity praying at the altar of Notre Dame des Victoires he would say to her: "My good Sister, I love to see you in my church, but it is your own chapel which should be the place of pilgrimage, because Our Lady showed herself there."

As we have said, the cures and conversions attributed to the Miraculous Medal number in their thousands, but one there is of special interest, both from its dramatic character and its far-reaching consequences: the conversion of Alphonse Ratisbonne.

Fr Alphonse Ratisbonne.

Alphonse Ratisbonne

The Ratisbonnes were a well-known Jewish family of Strasbourg, one of whom, Theodore, greatly to the dismay of his family, had become a Catholic and a priest. His greatest wish was that his youngest brother, Alphonse, should also become a Catholic. When Theodore was appointed director of the Association of Notre Dame des Victoires, he constantly asked for the prayers of the confraternity for this intention. Alphonse was travelling in Italy and finally went to Rome. Here everything he saw increased his scorn for Catholicism - churches, shrines, the piety of the people, all jarred on him. One day, he called on M. de Bussière, a zealous and enthusiastic convert, and at once got into a heated argument with him about religion. Alphonse Ratisbonne several times said that he had been born a Jew and a Jew he would die. Suddenly Bussière felt impelled to give him a Miraculous Medal and beg him to wear it. Ratisbonne, surprised, refused, but his friend persisted. "Why should you object?" he asked. "According to your way of thinking it can make no difference to you, whereas your wearing it would give me the greatest pleasure." "Oh, well," replied Ratisbonne, "if you put it like that, I'll take it, if only to show Jews are not as obstinate as we are supposed to be. Anyway," he added, "it will be an amusing item in my journal." But Bussière wasn't finished. Next, he gave him a copy of the Memorare saying: "I have another favour to ask you. Will you take this prayer and say it?" This was too much for Ratisbonne who turned away; but Bussière persisted, begging him at least to make a copy of the prayer. "Oh, all right," said Ratisbonne at last, intensely irritated; "I'll keep your copy and send you back mine." And off he went saying to himself: "What a tactless persistent fellow. What would he have said if I had tried to force Jewish prayers on him?"

M. de Bussière at once set about organising a campaign of prayers for the conversion of his friend, and he especially enlisted a saintly friend, M. de la Ferronnays, who took up the cause with enthusiasm.

A conversion

Ratisbonne, as he had promised, made a copy of the prayer and from that moment he could not get the words out of his mind. Day and night they haunted him. A few days later he met Bussière who told him that M. de la Ferronnays had died suddenly, to the grief of his many friends, and that he, Bussière, was on his way to the church of Sant' Andrea delle Fratte to make arrangements for the funeral. He asked Ratisbonne to wait for him there, and left him looking round the church. When Bussière returned, he couldn't see Ratisbonne anywhere, and thought he must have got bored and left. He was about to set out to find him when, to his astonishment, he saw him on his knees, deep in prayer, in one of the side-chapels. He went up and spoke to him, but Ratisbonne paid no attention, till at last he looked up, tears streaming down his face, and exclaimed: "Oh, how your friend must have prayed for me! Take me where you will," he added, "after what I have seen, I am obliged to obey." And drawing the medal from his breast, he kissed it, saying repeatedly: "Oh how good God is! What wonderful blessings! How happy I am!" Then, still apparently half-dazed, he asked his friend: "I'm not going mad, am I? No, I know what I am saying. I know I'm sane." Bussière saw clearly that something wonderful had happened, but the only answer he got to his anxious enquiries was "Take me away. Only on my knees can I tell what I have seen." So they went to see Fr de Villefort, a Jesuit, before whom Ratisbonne fell upon his knees. He again took out his medal and, kissing it with renewed fervour, cried: "I have seen her! I have seen her!" He then described what had happened: "I had been in the church a short time, when I was seized with extraordinary emotion. I looked up. The whole building seemed to have disappeared and the light was concentrated in one chapel. In the midst of this radiance, standing on the altar, appeared the Blessed Virgin Mary, tall, bright, majestic, full of tenderness, exactly as on my medal. An irresistible force drew me to her. She made a sign that I was to kneel down, and it seemed to me she said, 'That is right.' She did not speak to me, but I understood everything."

It did indeed appear that in that short moment Our Lady had taught him everything, for he seemed to need no more instruction. His one desire was for baptism. The Jews who had been converted by the Apostles had been baptised, he said; how could anyone refuse him, who had been converted by the Queen of the Apostles? Soon after he was baptised, he met the Holy Father, Pope Gregory XVI. "Nothing could exceed his kindness," said Ratisbonne. "He showed me, hanging near his bed, a beautiful picture of my dear medal to which he has a great devotion. I had brought with me a number of miraculous medals which His Holiness kindly blessed. They are the weapons I am going to use for the conversion of souls."

There was much joy, too, in Notre Dame des Victoires, where Fr Theodore related the story of the miracle. Alphonse Ratisbonne became a Jesuit, but later joined his brother in founding the Congregation of Our Lady of Sion, to bring Jews to Christianity. These days, the Congregation works for greater understanding between Jews and Christians.

Sister Catherine's Hidden Life

And what, all this time, of Sister Catherine? Amid the
glories of the medal she has faded from our eyes - as
indeed she would have wanted. While the wonders of the
Miraculous Medal were spoken of by everyone, the Sister
to whom it had been revealed was carrying on her humble,
active life, self-effacing and hard working; serving the old
men in the hospice; managing the dairy and the poultry
yard where, as of old, pigeons came answering to her
call, hovering round the white wings of her cornette (the
distinctive starched head-dress that marked out her order),
as once they had fluttered about the little farm girl. She
loved her work, especially the more lowly tasks, of which
she would allow no one to relieve her. "They are the pearls
of the Daughter of Charity," she would say. She never
wanted to go out. One spot alone attracted her - the chapel
of the mother house where her dear Lady had appeared
to her. And still she faithfully preserved her silence. She
shared her secret with Our Lady; it was not hers to break
the confidence. So not even Alphonse Ratisbonne, who
greatly desired to see her, nor Mgr de Quelen himself,
could change her mind. The Archbishop sent a message
through Fr Aladel: "If she wishes to remain hidden she

could surely cover herself with a veil and let me speak to her!" Once more, Our Lady came to her assistance by causing all memory of the heavenly visitation to vanish temporarily from her mind.

Doing her duty

A few among the Sisters guessed the truth, and she was sometimes hard put to it to baffle them. Two pictures of the apparitions were painted for the chapel, and Fr Aladel arranged for her to come and see them one day when he was present. Another Sister happened to come in at that moment and, struck by Sister Catherine's expression, exclaimed: "So this is the sister who had the vision!" Fr Aladel, taken by surprise, was silent, and left it to Sister Catherine to deal with the situation. "So you have found out my secret at last," she said with a merry laugh, but so simply that the other Sister was quite put off the scent. In all other respects Sister Catherine was in no way remarkable, for her perfection consisted in just doing her duty. That she should do the right thing at the right time and in the right way was quite simply taken for granted. One of her companions wrote later:

Having spent six years with Sister Catherine and worked for a year continually beside her, it would seem that I could tell a number of interesting and edifying details, but I am forced to admit that her life was so simple and so regular, that I can find nothing to remark on. Despite the secretly growing suspicion that she was the Sister so privileged by Our Lady, I scarcely believed it, her life was so little different from the rest of us. Sometimes I sought to find out indirectly by questioning her as to the impression made in the novitiate by the story of so wonderful an event, hoping that she would betray herself in her reply and satisfy my curiosity, but she would answer with such simplicity that my hopes were always frustrated.

Calm and acceptance

Always self-possessed and patient, she would often restrain the enthusiasm of the younger Sisters. "Sister, there's no need to get excited," she would say. They could see little of the long fight she had waged against her own self-will before attaining the outward calm that now seemed so natural to her. She made no display of piety - there were others in the house who seemed more devout. Her companions noticed only two things - her deep affection for the rosary, and the fact that when she prayed her eyes were always fixed upon the statue of Our Lady. As she grew older and her infirmities increased she would quite simply accept any slight alleviations that were offered her, but at the same time it seemed that feasts of Our Lady always brought her some special trial or suffering. One year, on the feast of the Immaculate Conception, several of the Sisters visited the mother house. On the way back, Sister Catherine fell whilst getting into the bus and broke her wrist. She said nothing till the Superior, seeing the way she was holding her arm, asked her what the matter was. "Oh, Sister," she answered, "it is only my bouquet I am holding. Every year Our Lady sends me one like this."

After her death some notes were found of her annual retreats. They were solid and practical and contained no mention of any special favours. The following are a few extracts:

I will take Mary as my model at the beginning of all my actions. In everything I will consider: If Mary were doing this, how would she do it? With what intention? Oh, how beautiful and consoling is the name of Mary!

Never to complain of the little contradictions I may meet with among the poor and to pray for those who make me suffer anything. O Mary, obtain this grace for me by your virginal purity.

In my temptations and times of dryness I will always have recourse to Mary, who is purity itself. O Mary, conceived without sin, pray for us who have recourse to you.

Humility, charity, simplicity, are the foundations of our holy vocation. O Mary, give me to understand these holy virtues. St Vincent, pray, pray for me. O

Mary, conceived without sin, pray, pray for me. Deign, O Queen of angels and of men, to look favourably on "the entire world and especially on France and on each individual in particular". O Mary, inspire us what we should ask of you for our own welfare and that of the whole world.

Finding consolation

So, for forty-six years, Sister Catherine led her hidden uneventful life at Enghien. In all her joys and sorrows she had only one refuge. Our Lady had once said to her, pointing to the tabernacle: "My daughter, in all your troubles, it is there you must find consolation." And Sister Catherine had faithfully obeyed. It didn't matter how harassed she might be, a few moments in the chapel never failed to restore peace to her soul and serenity to her countenance. After Fr Aladel's death, seeing that she, too, was beginning to fail, the Superior-General sent for her, wishing to take down a statement from her own lips. On her return, for the first time she opened her heart to Sister Dufes, then Superior at Enghien. This seemed to relieve her greatly, and from then on the Sisters noticed that she grew gentler, as though she no longer felt the same need to restrain her feelings. She often talked to Sister Dufes.

"I was only an instrument," she would say. "It was not for my own sake that Our Lady appeared to me. I knew nothing, not even how to write. All I know I have learnt in the community, and it is for that very reason that Our Lady chose me, so that no one could possibly have any doubts."

Sister Catherine was now seventy years of age and she felt her end was near. Although still devoted to her beloved old people and her almost equally beloved pigeons, she would assure the Sisters, as each of the great feasts came round: "This is the last time I shall keep this feast with you." Gradually her health gave way and she had to give up her active duties, one by one, till at last she was obliged to take to bed. Asthma and a heart condition rapidly undermined her strength. One day Sister Dufes asked her if she was afraid to die. "Afraid?" she said. "How can you think I should be afraid? I am going to find Our Lord, Our Lady, and St Vincent."

One of the Superiors of her Order came to visit her and, after talking for some time about the needs of the community, she said: "And now, Sister Catherine, when you get to heaven, you won't forget all this, will you? You will carry out what I've asked you, won't you?" "Sister, I'm only too willing," answered Sister Catherine, "but I've always been so stupid and so silly. I don't know how I shall be able to explain it all, since I don't know how they talk in heaven." "Dear Sister," said the other, smiling, "in heaven they don't speak as we do on earth. The soul looks at God and God looks at the soul and everything is understood. That's the language of heaven." "Oh, in that case," answered Sister Catherine, her face radiant, "you need have no fear. What you've asked will most certainly be accomplished."

A soul given to God

Another time, some of her former companions came to see her, among them one of the heads of the novitiate. "Sister, dear," she said sadly, "are you really going away without saying a single word to me about Our Lady?" The dying Sister Catherine drew her close and whispered in her ear: "The Father Superior has charge of that. I may not speak of it." And then she added: "But Our Lady is grieved because enough is not made of the treasure she has confided to the community in the devotion to the Immaculate Conception, and especially because the rosary is not well said. Our Lady has promised to grant special favours each time she is prayed to in the chapel - above all an increase of purity - that purity of spirit, of heart, of will, which is pure love."

At four o'clock one afternoon, the community were summoned to her deathbed. She lingered on till seven, and then, without the slightest struggle or the least sign of suffering, she gave her soul to God.

"We scarcely realized when she ceased to live," said Sister Dufes. "Never have I seen so calm and beautiful a death. And then the veil of humility under which she had so long sheltered was torn aside and this chosen soul so privileged by heaven was revealed to us. For now began the triumph of humility. The humble Sister whom none had noticed during life was after death surrounded by crowds of all ages and conditions who regarded it as the greatest happiness to be allowed to come, not to pray for her, but to beg her intercession."

A long procession followed her body to Reuilly, where she was laid to rest, accompanied by the prayer Our Blessed Lady taught her: "O Mary conceived without sin, pray for us who have recourse to you."

Nor was this the end. Truly, "he has exalted the humble". Sixty years later, on 28th May 1933, Pope Pius XI with some forty thousand of the faithful knelt in homage in St Peter's before the unveiled portrait of Catherine Labouré, as she was beatified. In the words of Christ's own Mother, "from henceforth all generations shall call me blessed."

"We do not know of any more striking example of the hidden life," said the Holy Father to seven thousand Children of Mary on this happy occasion, "than that of this soul of whom the whole world was speaking during her lifetime and for so many years, and who yet remained within the shadows, hidden with Jesus and Mary: hidden with Christ in God."

His Holiness Pope Pius XII, speaking to the crowds in St Peter's on the day, fourteen years later, of Sister Catherine's canonisation, recalled the words of his predecessor and presented this saint, who loved to remain unknown, as someone worthy of our imitation and another intercessor for us to appeal to in Heaven.

We could say that the year 1830, when the Virgin appeared to St Catherine, inaugurated the age of the Immaculate Conception. In 1854, in response to the prayer of the entire Church, Pope Pius IX defined the dogma of the Immaculate Conception, and a few years later the Immaculate Queen herself appeared at Lourdes. But while we hasten to obey her summons to go there as pilgrims, and rejoice in the ever-growing miracle of Lourdes, let us not neglect that earlier token of her love, the Miraculous Medal, through which she continues to work even today.

St Catherine Labouré on Prayer

Whenever I go to the chapel, I put myself in the presence of our good Lord, and I say to him, "Lord, I am here. Tell me what you would have me do." If he gives me some task, I am content and I thank him. If he gives me nothing, I still thank him since I do not deserve to receive anything more than that. And then I tell God everything that is in my heart. I tell him about my pains and joys, and then I listen. If you listen, God will also speak to you, for with the good Lord, you have both to speak and to listen. God always speaks to you when you approach him plainly and simply.

References

La Médaille Miraculeuse by Fr Aladel.

The Miraculous Medal by Lady Georgiana Fullerton (London, Burns & Oates, 1880).

A world of Catholic reading at your fingertips...

Catholic Faith, Life & Truth for all